THE CASTLE OF
NEUSCHWANSTEIN

OFFICIAL GUIDE

revised by

MICHAEL PETZET

and

GERHARD HOJER

1982

Bayerische Verwaltung der staatlichen Schlösser,
Gärten und Seen, München

Revised by Michael Petzet and Gerhard Hojer according to texts by Hans Thoma, which are essentially based on the 1933 edition of the Official Guide, revised by Heinrich Kreisel — Translation by Rudolf A. Gräter. — cover: Herpich OHG (Munich). - Photographs: Bayerische Verwaltung der staatl. Schlösser, Gärten und Seen (1, 2, 5, 6, 7, 8, 9, 10, 11, 13, 15, 16). — Werner Neumeister Munich (3, 4, 12, 14). — Illustrations pp. 3, 19 from "Gartenlaube" 1886, pp. 515, 617; illustrations pp. 14, 35 from a separate supplement of the "Neue Badische Landeszeitung", 1886. — Alphabetical index of artists and craftsmen by Alois Frisch.

For further information see:

Heinrich Kreisel, Die Schlösser Ludwig II. von Bayern, Franz Schneekluth, Darmstadt 1955. — Hans Rall/Michael Petzet, König Ludwig II., München 1968. — Michael Petzet, König Ludwig II. und die Kunst, Prestel-Verlag, München 1968 (with detailed list of sources and bibliography). — Detta and Michael Petzet, Die Richard Wagner-Bühne König Ludwigs II., Prestel-Verlag, München 1970. — English editions: Werner Richter, The Mad Monarch, the Life and Time of Ludwig of Bavaria, Henry Regnery Company, Chicago 1954. — Wilfried Blunt, The Dream King, Ludwig II of Bavaria, George Rainbird Ltd., London 1970. — Sigrid Russ, Die Ikonographie der Wandmalereien in Schloß Neuschwanstein, phil. Diss., Heidelberg 1974 (Manuscript); Gerhard Hojer und Horst Stierhof, Louis II de Bavière - L'art et le rêve, Brüssel 1977. — Sigrid Ruß, Bayerische Königsschlösser, München 1977. — Gerhard Hojer und Simon Jervis, Designs for the Dream King, London und New York 1978. — Schloß Neuschwanstein, Museum, Januar 1979. - Michael Petzet und Werner Neumeister, Die Welt des Bayerischen Märchenkönigs - Ludwig II. und seine Schlösser, München 1980. - Georg Baumgartner, Königliche Träume - Ludwig II. und seine Bauten, München 1981.

Reprint of the 1972 edition

311th – 360th Tsd.

Copyright by Bayerische Verwaltung der staatlichen Schlösser, Gärten und Seen, München
Printed in Germany
Rittel-Offset, Ortlerstraße 8, 8000 München 70

Neuschwanstein at the time of the death of Ludwig II, 1886.
Engraving by R. Assmus

KING LUDWIG II.
AND THE CASTLE OF NEUSCHWANSTEIN

The King announced the construction of the "New Castle of Hohen-schwangau" — (its name was changed to Neuschwanstein in the year of the death of Ludwig II) — in a letter to his friend Richard Wagner: "I intend to rebuild the old ruined castle of Hohenschwangau next to the Poellat-gorge. The style will be that of the original German knight's castles. The location is one of the most beautiful to be found: Holy and unapproachable, a worthy temple for our godly friend, who has bestowed upon mankind unique salvation and true blessing. It will remind you of the Tannhaeuser saga (Singer's Hall with view of the castle in the background) and the Lohengrin saga (courtyard with open passage and path to the chapel). This castle shall be more splendid and habitable than the lower castle of Ho-henschwangau, which every year is desecrated by the prose of my mother. The violated Gods cannot but seek revenge; they will stay with us way up here, breathing the air of heaven."

The King, after the frustrations of his first years on the throne, turned away in disgust from the residence town of Munich and took refuge in his beloved mountains. At Hohenschwangau "that para-dise on earth, that is alive with my ideals and makes me happy" he felt harassed by the "prose" of his mother, Queen Marie, who would not appreciate his ideals. Therefore the young King con-templated constructing a new dwelling in an environment, that was familiar to him since the days of his childhood. His father, Maximi-lian II, whose throne Ludwig ascended when he was eighteen, had, while still successor to the throne, purchased the ruined castle of Schwanstein in 1832, formerly the ancestral seat of the Knights of Schwangau. The place was intended to be rebuilt "in its original medieval style" according to plans drawn up by Domenico Quaglio, a decor painter. Ludwig intended renovating the ruins of Vorderhohenschwangau in exactly that style. The ruined castle was located on a hill East of Hohenschwangau called "Jugend". The same hill had seen the ruins of the castle of Hinterschwangau, one tower of which — the "Sylphenturm"— had been transformed into a visto pavillon by Maximilian II. In construction documents of 1868, reconstruction is still called "Restoration of the old castle ruins". Instead of restoration, a square tower and the walls of the old Palas were torn down to allow for the construction of the new Keep and the new Palas. Two ideas had seized the imagination of the young King; the typical late romantic fancy of restoration, which comes up again in 1883 in Ludwig's plans for the castle of Falkenstein, joins hands with the idea of a new castle of the Swanknight Lohengrin. The arms of Lohengrin are repeatedly seen in the castle of Ludwig's father, one that had considerable bearing on Ludwig's appreciation of art. The swan had also been the favourite animal of Maximilian II.

The arrival of Ludwig's beloved hero on the Alpsee was the typical prelude to the construction of the new castle. Young prince Ludwig had become familiar with the Lohengrinsaga as painted on the walls of his father's castle, long before he had his fateful experience with Richard Wagner's opera of the same name which he saw performed by the Munich Royal Opera on February 2, 1861. When Wagner himself stayed at Hohenschwangau Castle between November 11th and 18th, 1865, he arranged that the 'morning call' of the Lohengrin opera was played from several towers of the castle by the oboe players of the first Infantry Regiment. When "the days of bliss" at the castle ended, those unique days of harmonious friendship between King and composer, Ludwig ordered a display of fireworks followed by a performance of special significance, for it was given directly beneath the ancestral home of the knights of Schwangau. The event was recorded in the chronicle of Hohenschwangau: "In the evening of November 21 splendid fireworks were displayed,

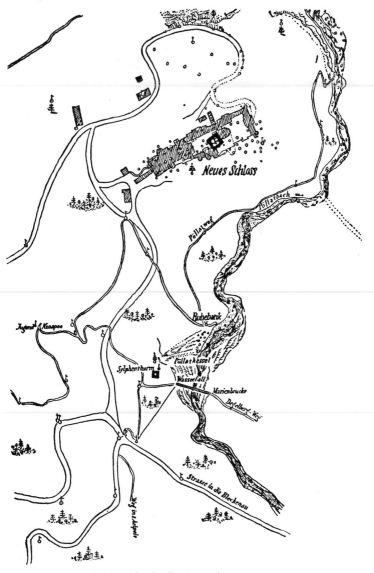

Section of a landregister plan (1868)
with the ruins of Vorderhohenschwangau (Neues Schloß)
and Hinterhohenschwangau (Sylphenturm)

perfectly coordinated by Penkmayr, a theatretechnician. Following this, the arrival of the Swanknight was staged in the scenery of the Alpsee: A huge, ingenously built swan was towing Lohengrin's boat (Aide-de camp Prince Paul von Thurn and Taxis acted as Lohengrin) across the lake. Swanknight, swan and boat were all beautifully illuminated by electrical lights, and an orchestra played respective musical motives from the Lohengrin opera. The scene was repeated again the following evening by orders of the King." Later the King would occasionally enjoy playing the role of Lohengrin himself. Thus, year before the laying of the foundationstone of Neuschwanstein on September 5, 1869, Ludwig had realised the first act, of the Lohengrin opera, "on the banks of the Schelde river". The décor of the opera's second act — "courtyard of the castle of Antwerp" — provided Christian Jank, a décor painter who had drawn the first sketches for Neuschwanstein, with a model for the future courtyard; this model can easily be traced to Angelo II Quaglio's designs for the performance of Lohengrin in Munich in 1867. The same was true with plans for a bedroom in the Kemenate (ladies bower) which were taken from the setting of the opera's third act, they were, however, never put to use. The letter to Wagner, quoted above, proves that Ludwig intended Neuschwanstein to be the castle of Lohengrin as well as that of Tannhaeuser. Upon the suggestion of Wagner Ludwig and his brother travelled incognito to Wartburg castle near Eisenach on May 31, 1867 (the castle being the historical stage of "the Singers' Contest"), to prepare a new production of Tannhaeuser. The same year had seen the completion of the reconstruction of that castle. The journey proved successful in two ways: Heinrich Döll, a landscape specialist among Munich's décor painters, came up with a drawing for the first and third act of Tannhaeuser that showed a historically exact replica of the Wartburgcastle, set in the background of the Wartburg valley. At the same time King Ludwig went ahead with plans for building Neuschwanstein on the rugged cliffs above the Poellat-gorge. An adaptation of the Singers' Hall of the Wartburgcastle was initially part of the project. Though completed only in 1867, its plans had been used by special orders of King Friedrich Wilhelm IV of Prussia as décor for the second act of the first production of Tannhaeuser in Berlin as early as 1858. Jank drew his ideas for the actual singers' hall from two sources: the Festive Hall and the 'historical' Singers' Hall of the Wartburg castle. Future settings for Tannhaeuser performances were adopted from Jank's design of the new singers' hall. Since the castle was to include all the scenes of Lohengrin and Tannhaeuser there was only one still lacking: the "Grotto of the Hörselberg". Hohenschwangau, the castle built by Ludwig's father, Maximilian II, already boasted of a rather peculiar kind of cave pool lined with red marble. The original plans for Neuschwanstein include a great grotto in the basement of the castle; though it was never realised, the idea emerged again in 1875 and led to the construction of the grotto of Venus at Linderhof Castle. At Neuschwanstein a small grotto was instead built next to the King's study.

Eduard Riedel, an architect who had renovated the Berg Castle between 1849 and 1851, was to design construction plans according to the pictorial views drawn by Christian Jank. In 1868, under Riedel's supervision, the site was levelled and the construction of a road began. The plans for the future castle were finally completed. The project already included the Kemenate, the Knights' House, the Communicating Building and the Gateway Building, The King felt it to be desirable to substitute the concept of a "robber knight castle" of Nuremberg late gothic stylistic elements with the concept of a monumental "romanesque" castle. The Palas of the new castle was intended to remind us of the Wartburg Palas. Future designs of Jank reflected the King's change of mind. Though oddly enough, commonly considered to be the essence of a medieval castle, Neuschwanstein is actually a typical creation of "Historicism", the world-wide revival of interest in earlier architectural forms. Jank's project was criticized by orthodox romantics who would rather have preferred copies and combinations of historical buildings. The castellan of the Wartburg castle recommended that

Ludwig employed the painter Michael Welter to work out the "necessary details" needed to achieve a true replica of romanesque style. Welter was sure that Jank's designs would inevitably "incite the most malicious and bitter comments." In a letter dated November 21, 1871, court secretary Düfflipp turned down Welter's recommendations with reasons that reveal his manner of thinking: "His Majesty, the King, wishes the castle to be built in the romanesque style. Do I have to remind you that we are living in the year 1871, centuries after the period that created the romanesque style. I think we should not neglect the achievements of the Arts and Sciences. On the contrary, one ought to apply them to ones' advantage. — We will not accept any change as far as the character of the style is concerned, but there is no need for turning back the clock and forget experiences that would have been used then if only known."

Only the gateway-building completed in 1873, is reminiscent of gothic forms. When Georg Dollmann became Riedel's successor in 1874, construction and ornamentation grew more and more frugal and many picturesque details of Jank's designs were dropped. Construction that followed increased this tendency because little was completed by 1886, the year of Ludwig's death: Only the Palas was well on the way to completion and its exteriors were at least finished. The work at the Knight's House had begun in 1882, but by 1886 it still was bare brick work. The same was true of the Communicating Building. Still worse, construction of the Kemenate and the Keep had just been started. Only the Kemenate was later completed; construction of the Keep that was to overlook the whole site, soon ceased. In the years between 1886 and 1892, under the supervision of Julius Hofmann, the castle was more or less completed. While Dollmann was still the headarchitect at the site, Hofmann had put the finishing touch on the Palas. The latter was designated to succeed Dollmann in 1884, and at this time took charge of al royal buildings. Hofmann was a skilled architect who had helped his father with the construction of Archduke Maximilian's castle at Miramare near Trieste. In 1864, he was sent to Mexico by order of the Archduke to convert Mexico City's Townhall into a residence for the future Emperor. For Neuschwanstein he had designed the entire 'romanesque' interior decoration according to the King's ideas; like a "Leitmotiv", the swan appears repeatedly. Only the interior decoration of Ludwig's bedroom and the chapel next to it originally designed by Peter Herwegen, display a 'late gothic' style in decoration and furniture that comes closer to 'historical' forms than the "Biedermeier" neogothic style of Hohenschwangau.

The King himself was keenly interested in every small detail of the interior and frequently ordered corrections to be made before work could begin. He devoted special attention to the planning of the mural paintings. When Ludwig was still a child, his father had Hohenschwangau painted with murals of regional myths, some of them designed by Moritz von Schwind. Dr. Hyazinth Holland, a historian of literature, and specialist in medieval iconography, furnished Ludwig with a collection of various suggestions as to the decoration of the future castle. Since Ludwig intended the castle a "temple" in Wagner's honour (according to the above quoted letter) he chose almost exclusively motives from Wagner operas. Ludwig, however, was determined to return to the historical roots of Wagner's work and ordered in 1879: "The paintings of the new castle ought to revive the real sagas and not Wagner's interpretations of them." Ludwig required "painters who are extraordinarily familiar with medieval poetry" and who would, by virtue of their aquaintance with literature, reflect the King's spiritual conception — a conception based on a true or imagined and poetically glorified "historical truth". Any exaggeration was condemned as a farçe. Naturally, there could not be any place for "profanities" in this kind of historical depiction. The King, very conscious of his own dignity, demanded a manner of representation that was at the same time "elevated" and "natural". That did not improve matters and the significance of some of the works can only be seen as being an integrating part of Neuschwanstein as a 'total work of art'. Ludwig hated "the well-known dilatoriness of artists" and set up a deadline that was nearly impossible to meet; he ordered the paintings of his apartments to be finished by Christmas day of 1881. Working desperately day and night, Hauschild, Spieß, Piloty, Aigner, and Ille, the artists, succeeded in fulfilling the King's orders.

Later the program of Neuschwanstein had to be altered frequently to meet the changing ideas of the King. Years before the first performance of "Parsifal" at Bayreuth, Ludwig concerned himself with the opera's décor. In 1876 Eduard Ille was asked to design a Grail Hall in the Byzantine style, adapted from the Hagia Sophia in Istanbul. Ludwig carried the idea further and arrived at the concept of a Neuschwanstein "Thronsaal" (throne hall) that is reminiscent of the All Saints Church Munich. The idea was realized according to plans drawn up by Julius Hofmann in 1881. Thus the castle of Lohengrin and Tannhaeuser, designed for the young King, was converted into Parsifal's "castle of the Grail", in which the ageing King pleaded for his redemption. The six canonized Kings, painted in the Apse of the throne hall, plead for the cause of a veritable monarchy by God's grace. Their deeds are depicted in frescoes carried out mainly by Wilhelm Hauschild. The original plans for the Singer's Hall were modified; it was now supposed to introduce to the throne hall and was decorated with mural paintings which presented the Parzival saga according to Wolfram von Eschenbach. In the singer's bower Parzival appears as the King of the Holy Grail, and the departure of his son, Lohengrin, is on the opposite wall. Thus the concept of Neuschwanstein is united at start and finish in the saga of the Swan-knight.

The throne hall is the King's only project of Byzantine style that was, with the exception of the throne itself, completed by the time he died. Dollman in 1869 and later Hofmann in 1885 designed huge Byzantine palaces which were supposed to manifest, as is shown in Herrenchiemsee in a different way, Ludwig's monarchy by God's grace. Since Falkenstein castle near Pfronten, and many other projects, were never carried beyond the planning stage, Neuschwanstein remains in many respects a unique monument to one of the most creative members of the Wittelsbach House. His works gained their individual quality from their connection with the theatre — Neuschwanstein from Wagner's operas, Linderhof, Herrenchiemsee and the 'oriental' buildings from the famous private performances. As a major work of "Historicism", Neuschwanstein shows — not to mention the important benefits for the arts and crafts of Munich — the creative achievements of 19th century art; they range from baffling harbingers of "art nouveau", as seen in Jank's designs for the colonnades of the Knight's House or in the details of the throne hall's 'romanesque' chandeliers, to such amazingly "modern" solutions as single-pane windows and a sliding door also made of a single piece of glass leading to the Conservatory. In addition, the King's projects reveal the application of the most modern technical devices of the time. Striking examples are the skillfully furnished kitchen at Neuschwanstein or the electrical powerplant in the Linderhof grotto.

The king lived in his apartments at Neuschwanstein for the first time in 1884 between May 27 and June 8. While Maximilian II and Ludwig I built principally for the public, Ludwig II's castles and palaces were so exclusively reserved for the King himself that he could cherish the idea of their destruction after his death. For him the castles were more than a mere illusory world into which he withdrew in protest against the bourgeois world which showed no understanding of him: they were his very life, in which dream and reality were blended and history lived again — not merely on a stage. Here the King acted with an extreme skill and energy which he completely lacked in political matters; in no way did he ruin the State Treasury by his untertakings, as is often alleged, but paid everything out of his own private purse. But when the privy purse ran heavily into debt and building had to stop, the King's life lost its purpose. On June 12, 1886, a Government Commission took him from Neuschwanstein to Berg. Thus Ludwig, despairing of the vocation of a monarch within a constitutional monarchy, finally had to perish, because, as he wrote once to Wagner, in an "ideal, monarchical, poetical solitude" he had tried to create an art in harmony with his personal view of the universe. In 1886, when all of Europe was shaken by his dramatic death in the Lake Starnberg, Paul Verlaine called him the "only true king of the century".

King Ludwig II on a sleigh-ride from Hohenschwangau to Berg, 1886

THE CASTLE

The Castle of Neuschwanstein (3306 feet above sea-level) is built in the style of the late romanesque period of the early 13th century. This style is obvious in the construction of the building as a whole as well as in its ornamentation: the round arched portals, the arcade windows and towers, the position of columns and its baywindows and pinnacles.

To the east is the Gateway Building, to the south the "Kemenate", to the north the Communicating Building containing the Knights' House and the Square Tower, and to the west the "Palas". The whole building is plated with square labs of limestone from a near-by quarry.

Exterior

Northern Front (as seen from the last bend of the mountain road), from left to right, the Northern Corner Tower of the Gateway Building, Lower Communicating Building, Square Tower Upper Communicating Building, Knights' House with tower containing staircase, northern front of the east part of the Palas with Conservatory, Rectangular Tower containing staircase, balcony of the Study and Octagonal Tower containing staircase (213 feet) and northern front of the throne hall.

Stone-sculptures: At the Rectangular Tower, statue of the Madonna; at the Octagonal Tower the figure of St. George, both done by Ph. Perron.

Western Front: (as seen from the road leading to Mary's bridge)

The western gable has two turrets on either side and in the center a knight's statue. The door to the groundfloor was intended to lead on to a large terrace never realized. On this site some of the foundations of the medieval ruin of Vorderhohenschwangau are still to be seen. Balcony patterned after the Wartburg; lower part: Balcony of the Moorish Hall which was never completed; upper part: Balcony of the throne hall with arcades.

Sculptures: Statue of St. Cecilia at the north-western corner. — Copper embossed knight statue with lion shield (possibly Otto von Wittelsbach).

Southern Front (as seen from Mary's bridge)

Most impressive view of the Castle situated high above the steep rocks of the Poellat gorge, in the background the plains near Fuessen. From left to right: Palas with Round Tower containing staircase and the bay window and balcony of the bedroom, the Kemenate with Square Tower containing staircase and projecting octagonal center part. Bridged-over gorge underneath the "Kemenate". — The southeastern part of the site was never completed, thus allowing a view of the keep and of the Gateway Building.

Eastern Front (as seen from the entrance)

Two-storied crenelated Gateway Building with round corner towers and a three storied center part with a gable. Walls lined with bricks and sand-stone. Above the entrance the Bavarian royal coat of arms, above this a gallery which widens at the corners into two balconylike projections.

Courtyards

Lower Courtyard

To the east the Gateway Building, to the north the Communicating Building (with an outside staircase leading to the Gateway Building)

16

and Square Tower, to the west a wall with a projecting center part, fountain, and outside staircase leading to the Upper Courtyard, and to the south a low wall to the Poellat gorge.

Gateway building: Barrel-vaulted-groined entrance passage. In the tympanum of the entrance to the guards' room a relief of a dog with the circumscription: "During day and night fidelity is vigilant." The façade of the courtyard is covered with limestone and the upper part with yellow and streaked sandstone from Bayreuth; a balcony with colonnades on the second floor of the center building, symbolic reliefs in the tympanums of the towers. Until 1884, when the rooms in the Palas were finished, the King inhabited the rooms of the second floor (now not accessible to the public) in order to supervise the construction work personally. In the rooms on the first floor the King, on June 10th, 1886, for a short time held captive the commission which was to place him under guardianship and proclaim a regency.

Square tower: Height 148 feet with a projecting gallery and a round top part with battlements.

Western revetment: The projecting polygonal section with buttresses was intended to become the foundation of the planned choir of the chapel. Above this keep was to be erected.

Upper Courtyard

To the west the gabled façade of the Palas, to the south the Kemenate, to the east the top part of the revetment of the Lower Courtyard, and to the north the two-storied Communicating Building with the three-storied Knight's House in the center.

Palas: A flight of stone steps leads to the portal, asymmetrically arranged on the right side of the first floor. At the upper part of the narrow six-storied gabled façade the balcony of the Singers' Hall, two frescos (St. George and the Patrona Bavariae) and two octagonal corner turrets; a copper-chased figure of a lion surmounts the gable.

Kemenate: Three-storied building. Walls subdivided with projecting sections. Projecting center section with portal and balcony above. Along the western section, stairs leading to a portal in the first floor. Erected after the King's death and finished in 1892. The façade, which was to be decorated with statues of female saints, was left plain; the interior decoration was never executed.

Keep on the East-side: The chapel with three aisles and polygonal closed choir was, like the Keep itself, never completed.

Communicating Building with Knights' House: Two-storied building, containing the passages which connect the Square Tower and the Palas, upper floor with double windows in blind arches. On the top of the long wing, Knight's House with gable. The intended rich architectural ornamentation designed by Chr. Jank in 1870 was not carried out.

Neuschwanstein seen from south-west, 1886.

INTERIOR OF THE PALAS

The King's living quarters and representational rooms in the third and fourth floor were more or less completed by 1886. The ornamental decoration of the Entrance Hall and the corridors was realised after 1888. The paintings in each room refer to the work of some medieval poet, whereas the two large lounges show scenes from the Gudrun und Sigurd saga.

First Floor

Entrance Hall and Corridor

The Entrance Hall is divided into two aisles. Groined vaults adorned with decorative paintings, floor covered with tiles from Mettlach. To the left of the corridor, behind round-arched double windows, are the servants' quarters.

Lounge

The form of this hall narrowing toward the windows is determined by the western wing, adjoined in an obtuse angle because of the rocky configuration of this site. It has a groined vaulted ceiling.

Decoration: Along the walls, benches with tooled leather cushions. — Wrought iron lanterns, like the lanterns in the winding staircase designed by J. Hofmann in 1833 and executed by K. Moradelli in 1884.

Winding staircase in the Northern Tower

On the column in the middle of the stairs a painted frieze with hunting scenes. Wrought iron lanterns, with pulleys to let down, decorated with dragons' heads.

Second Floor

Landing

The rooms on the second floor are still in bare brickwork and not accessible to the public. There, a large Moorish hall was intended and also a bathroom and some servants' rooms. Door with wrought iron mountings.

Third Floor

Landing

In the arched stained glass window above the door the coats of arms of Bavaria, Wittelsbach and Schwangau; door with glass and wrought iron bars.

The King's Apartments

1 Lounge

Shaped the same as the lounge on the first floor. Ceiling with groined vaults. On the eastern side, marble portal and two open double arches (leading to the King's apartments) and a narrow door (to the staircase in the Southern Tower); on the western side, marble portale opening to the throne hall. Scenes of the Sigurd saga painted on the walls. The Sigurd saga corresponds to the medieval Siegfried saga; it is the version as told in the "Edda", the oldest transmitted collection of Germanic legends.

Wall sculptures by Ph. Perron like in all rooms of the castle. Capitals decorated with knight's heads and animals; coats of arms of Bavaria and Schwangau at the keystons of the vault. Dragons on unpolished capitals of the pillars on the portal leading to the throne hall.

Murals by W. Hauschild in 1882. — *Sigurd saga:* The father of Fafnir and Regin had seized upon a mighty gold-treasure scorned by the gods. Fafnir usurps this "Nibelungen"-treasure after his father's death and guards it as a dragon. Regin, the dwarf, forges the famous sword "Gram" and hands it to Sigurd, the young king. Sigurd kills Fafnir and Regin to gain the cursed treasure. Sigurd rides through flames and finds the sleeping valkyrie Brynhild. They pledge love to each other. Travelling on, Sigurd arrives at the court of the Franconian King on the banks of the Rhine. His daughter Gudrun offers Sigurd a philtre that makes him forget Brynhild. Sigurd marries Gudrun and helps Gunnar, his brother-in-law, to win Brynhild. When the truth is revealed to Brynhild, she seeks revenge. Guttorm, Gunnar's youngest brother, must kill Sigurd. Brynhild stabs herself with a sword and is burnt with Sigurd on the same pyre. — Wall to the right: "Gripyn reveals Sigurd's fate." — "Regin forges the sword 'Gram' for Sigurd" — "Sigurd kills Fafnir" — "Sigurd riding through the fire to Brynhild". — Typanum above the window: "Gudrun offering the philtre to Sigurd". — Wall to the left (beginning at the window): "Sigurd's death" (with the three princes: Gunnar and Högni to the left, Guttorm to the right) — "Gudrun waiting for Sigurd's return" — "Brynhild scorning Gunnar". — At the entrance wall: "Gudrun laments the corpse of Sigurd" — "Sigurd's and Brynhild's bodies are burnt on the same pyre."

Decoration: Benches along the walls with cushions of tooled leather (arms of Bavaria, Wittelsbach and Schwangau). — Wrought iron chandeliers by K. Moradelli. — Red silk curtains made in Brussels.

2 Throne Hall

Two-storeyed hall in a churchlike sumptuous style influenced by Byzantine patterns and the Munich All Saints Church. Rectangular room with a gallery supported by columns (the lower part imitation porphyry, the upper part imitation lapis-lazuli) covered by a flattened cupola. At the north side, marble stairs leading to an apse, covered by a half-dome. Tesselated pavement with ornamental patterns, plants and animals. The pictures in the apse show "Christ in his glory", six canonized Kings, and the twelve Apostels; under the arcades paintings of the Saints' lives, the victory of St. George and of the archangel Michael. Paintings under the vault, entrance wall: motives of the Ancients, the Old Testament and Christianity. — Access to the balcony with a splendid view of mountains, lakes and low land.

History of construction: First sketches, by E. Ille from 1867—1877, are derived from a description of the Grail castle in "Titurel" by Albrecht von Scharfenberg (around 1260); final plans by J. Hofmann in 1884. Not completed on account of the King's death. The throne of gold and ivory with canopy and four life-sized angels holding the escutcheons of Bavaria, Wittelsbach, and Schwangau is missing. Paintings on the back wall of the apse done as late as 1886 after designs by E. Drollinger.

Tesselated pavement designed by A. Spenger in 1884, executed by Detoma (Vienna). — Stairs leading to the missing throne: Carrara marbel 'Bianco Chiaro'.

Murals on gold background by W. Hauschild and other artists. — Apse: "Christ in his glory, with St. John and Mary and angels", underneath in a friezelike arrangement six kings canonized for their services for christianity. From left to right: Kasimir, Prince of Poland and Elected King of Hungary, Stephen I of Hungary, Henry II of Germany, Louis IX of France, Ferdinand III of Spain, and Edward the Confessor, the Saxon King of England. At the side of the stairs the twelve Apostels. — Under the arcades, beginning from the entrance: "Edward the Confessor as a righteous knight" — "Ferdinand III of Spain fighting the Moors" — "St. George" — "Landgravine Elizabeth of Thuringia, occupied with charity work" — "Queen Clotilde of France converting her husband Clovis to christianity" — "Casimir of Poland praying at the altar". — Up in the arcades, beginning at the entrance: "The Hungarians' conversion to christianity by King Stephen I." — "Henry II of Germany laying the foundation stone of the Cathedral of Bamberg" — "The Archangel

Michael" — "King Louis IX of France feeding the poor". — Paintings under the vault, entrance wall: "The ancient law" (in the center the Roman law, to the left Zoroaster, to the right Solon). — Opposite: "The moral law of the Old Testament" (Moses with the Decalogue). — In the middle: "The law of the New Testament" (Adoration of the Three Wise Men). — Dome decorated with golden stars and luminous rays. In the corner spandrels, angels with the royal insignia.

Candelabra and chandelier of gilded brass designed by J. Hofmann in 1884, executed by E. Wollenweber. Chandelier (about 1900 lbs, 96 candles) with reliefs of ivory imitation.

Balcony: Exceptionally fine view of the surroundings of the castle. From left to right: the Saeuling (6691 feet above sea-level), Mary's Bridge (height above the Poellat gorge about 300 ft), Alpsee, Schwarzenberg, Schwansee, the plains around Fuessen, Hopfensee and Forggensee. — Legend reports that the Schwarzenberg is the dragon of the Nibelungen saga turned into stone. The form is still to be recognised: The hilltop with Hohenschwangau is the head, the castle represents the crown, the chain of hills itself is supposed to be the curved back with the haunches of the dragon, whose tail encircles the Alpsee.

3 *Anteroom*

Oak pannelling and coloured patterns on the walls, beamed cealing and, between corbels of the smaller walls, coats of arms.

Decoration: Simple furniture; upholstering of tooled pigskin. — Electrical bell system (1885): the system (current was supplied by a dry battery) allowed the King to call to a servant from an room of the Palas.

4 *Dining Room*

Above the carved oak panelling and the doors, paintings with scenes of the time of Landgrave Hermann of Thuringia, and minstrel portraits. Above the windows, allegorical pictures of knightly virtues.

Beamed ceiling with carved ornamentation. Oak furniture; on the dining table, a gilt bronze center-piece picturing Siegfried's fight with the dragon.

Murals and portraits above the doors by F. Piloty and J. Aigner. — Exit wall: "The Landgrave presents gifts to minstrels" — "Gottfried von Strasbourg" — "The Landgrave returns to Heinrich von Veldeke the poem 'Äneide', which had been lost." — Backwall: "Sorcerer Klingsor, dressed up as an oriental merchant, wants members of the court to solve his riddles" — "Wolfram von Eschenbach" — "Singer's contest at the Wartburg". — Entrance wall: "Klingsor takes Heinrich von Ofterdingen to the Wartburg" — "Reinmar von Zweter" — "The Landgrave asking Wolfram von Eschenbach to translate the poem 'Willehalm'". — Wall with windows: "Performance of minstrels at the Landgrave's court." — Fields of quatrefoil shape above the window-arches: "Prudence and Moderation" — "Justice and Bravery".

Decoration: On the dining table, gilt bronze center-piece, "Siegfried fighting with the dragon", done by E. Wollenweber in 1885—86 after a model by L. Bierling. — Coverings of gold embroidered red silk. — Coloured tiled stove. — Chandelier and candlestick of gilded brass by E. Wollenweber.

5 Bedroom

Just as in all his other castles the King wished the bedroom to be especially sumptuous. The style of this room is, in contrast to the other romanesque rooms, late Gothic. — Carved oak panels, big center pillar, ceiling of joisted wood work. The whole room is devoted to "Tristan and Isolde", a poem by Gottfried of Strasbourg. The mural paintings on gobelin fabrics show scenes of the poem and the clay figures on the corners of the tiled stove the main characters. Richly carved oak furniture: bed with an exquisite canopy and reading chair with canopy, toiletry cabinet, washstand and chairs. On the south wall, bay-window with carved wood panelled ceiling, and balcony offering a plendid view of the Poellat gorge.

History of construction: Basic designs by P. Herwegen in 1869; final plans by J. Hofmann in 1880—81.

Wooden sculptures: On the center pillar four minstrels, dwarfs supporting the middle beam. Above the exit, wooden figures of Tristan, King Marke and Isolde.

Murals by A. Spieß in 1881. — Entrance wall: "Tristan bids farewell to Isolde" — "Tristan expecting Isolde". — Wall with windows: "Isolde's arrival with Kurwenal". — Exit wall: "Tristan and Isolde united in death" — "Tristan offers Isolde the philtre" — In the arch: "Lady reading the Tristan saga". — Backwall: "Faithfulness" — "Tristan and Isolde in the gardens of the Cornwall castle" — "Love".

Stained glass bay-windows: Panes picturing the arms of Wittelsbach, Bavaria, and Schwangau.

Decoration: Oak furniture designed by J. Hofmann in 1881—82, made by A. Pössenbacher in 1883. Richly carved bed with a canopy, comparable to a Gothic building with numerous turrets. In front a relief of the resurrection of Christ. At the head of the bed a madonna painted on copper after a Byzantine original. — Washstand under canopy with swans. On the marble plate a silver swan as water tap and a silver basin to tilt. Wash set with water pitcher and spunge container of gilded bronze by E. Wollenweber, designs by J. Hofmann. — Reading chair: on the back, the arms of Bavaria and Schwangau. — Coverings and curtains embroidered with lions, swans, coats of arms, crowns, and fleurs-de-lis on blue silk, curtains by M. Steinmetz (1886). — Brown tiled stove with clay figures of Tristan and Isolde. — Neogothic chandelier and candle holders of gilded brass by E. Wollenweber (1883).

6 Oratory

Oak wood panelling with carved, neogothic ornamentation. The mural paintings, the paintings on the windows and the center of the triptych are devoted to St. Louis (Louis IX of France), the patron saint of Ludwig II.

History of construction: Designs for the decoration in 1880 by J. Hofmann.

Murals by W. Hauschild: "Death of St. Louis" — "St. Louis receives the Banner of the Cross."

Stained glass windows: "St. Louis receiving extreme unction", Mayersche Hofkunstanstalt (1882) after designs by J. Hofmann.

Decoration: Altar with paintings on gold by W. Hauschild: St. Louis in the center, angels on the inner side of the richly carved wings. On the altar, an ivory cross by A. Dießl. — Praying desk of oakwood made by A. Pössenbacher in 1883, covering of violet velvet with silver embroidery by M. Steinmetz.

7 Dressing Room

Above oak panelling, pictures on golden ground with scenes described in the poetry of Walther von der Vogelweide. Another painting shows Hans Sachs at the Nuremberg fairgrounds. Above the entrance to the bay-window, two frontal pictures of these medieval poets. The ceiling is painted sky-blue with clouds and birds, around the sides a trellis with clinging vine: The artist intends to give the impression of an open bower with the blue sky above. Inside the bay-window three motives of Hans Sachs' life. — Carved oak furniture, pottery toilet set, jewelry box.

History of construction: Interior designs by J. Hofmann in 1880—1881.

Murals by E. Ille, a pupil of famous Moritz von Schwind. — Entrance wall: "The birds teach Walther von der Vogelweide how to sing" — "Walther singing at the court of Duke Guelph". — Above the window: "Walther raising enthusiasm for the crusade." — On the wall behind the stove: "Walther with his fiddle riding from one castle to the other" — "The mastersinger Hans Sachs surrounded by his friends, among whom is Albrecht Duerer, Peter Vischer, Pirkheimer" (in the Background the castle of Nuremberg) — "Walther sitting on a stone, meditating." — Exit wall: "Walther on board the ship, partaking in the crusade" — "Under the linden-tree", an illustration of one of Walther's most beautiful lovepoems. — In the bay-window: "Hans Sachs handing the master's chain to a young mastersinger" — "Hans Sachs with his friends" — "Hans Sachs in his study."

Decoration: Jewelry box with painting showing the medieval "jus primae noctis" (seignorial right) by A. Spieß after J. A. Garnier. — On the washstand, a majolica toilet set by Villeroy & Boch-Mettlach 1882, designs by J. Hofmann. — Fabrics by M. Steinmetz in 1883: Coverings and curtains of violet silk with the peacock pattern in golden embroidery.

8 *Living Room*

This room is devoted to the Lohengrin saga, which in the King's imagination was especially related to the castle by the motive of the swan. The escutcheons at the top of the walls refer to this poem. Recess formed by arches and columns. Big bookcase with paintings, brass chandeliers and candle sticks adorned with Bohemian glass. On the tiled stove, a swan made of china serving as a vase. Blue silk curtains with the motive of the swan.

History of construction: Preliminary sketches in 1870 by P. Herwegen. Final plans for interior decorations and furniture by J. Hofmann in 1879 and 1881 respectively.

Columns: Capitals with frontal pictures of Jesus, an emperor, a bishop, and a crusading knight.

Murals by W. Hauschild, only the first one by A. von Heckel. — Northern wall: "Lohengrin's arrival." — Exit wall: "The miracle of the Grail" — "Lohengrin's departure from the castle of the Grail" (above the door) — "Lohengrin's landing at Antwerp" (in the alcove). — Backwall of the alcove: "Lohengrin greeting Elsa" — "Elsa telling Lohengrin her grief". — Wall to the right of the alcove: "Lohengrin's fight with Telramund". — Entrance wall: "Elsa asking the Question" — "Lohengrin on the journey home" (above the door). — All murals with rich ornamentation (interlaced vines, gem motives) on gold background. — Under the ceiling of the alcove: "Lohengrin's mission" — "Lohengrin and Elsa's wedding" (ceremony, bridal procession, and feast).

Pictures on the doors of the bookcase by F. Piloty. — From left to right: "Gottfried von Strasbourg, with lady and monk", above "Tristan and Isolde"; Wolfram von Eschenbach, the poet of "Parzival" and above, the

Grail with two angels; to the right, "The legendary blind poet of the 'Nibelungenlied' dictating his poem", above, "The dream of Krimhild".

Decoration: Blue silk curtains and coverings by M. Steinmetz (1883) with the swan motive and lilies embroidered. — Candlesticks and chandeliers of gilded brass by E. Wollenweber (1883).

9 Grotto and Conservatory

Grotto with artificial stalagmites and stalactites by the "landscape sculptor". A. Dirigl. Motive: Hörselberg of the Tannhaeuser saga. The grotto can be illuminated by coloured lights and originally there was a small cascade. The glass door offers a view of the Conservatory. Moorish fountain planned for the Moorish hall situated one storey lower but never completed.

10 Study

Divided in the same manner with columns as the anteroom. On the walls the Tannhaeuser saga painted on canvas by J. Aigner. Carved ceiling, Oak panelling and oak furniture made, as in adjoining rooms, in the Munich craft shops of A. Pössenbacher and A. Ehrengut. Glazed tiled stove.

Murals by J. Aigner. — Entrance wall: "Tannhaeuser travels to the Wartburg" — "Tannhaeuser at Venus' mountain abode" — "Tannhaeuser meets the Landgrave". — Back wall: "Tannhaeuser as penitent before the Pope Urban IV" — "Tannhaeuser as dance-musician". — Exit wall: "Singer's contest at the Wartburg" — "Tannhaeuser's arrival at the Wartburg". — Wall with windows: "Landgravine Elisabeth" — "Flute-playing shepherd boy in front of the Wartburg". — Murals inside the arches: "Tannhaeuser and Venus" — "Tannhaeuser as pilgrim." — Painting in the backdoor's tympanum: "Pegasus with Cupids".

Decoration: Bookcase to keep the sketches and plans of the castle designed by J. Hofmann in 1881. — On the desk, writing utensils executed by F. Harrach in 1883 after models by Ph. Perron. — Coverings of green silk with gold-embroidered lions and Bavarian coats of arms. Corresponding curtains by M. Jörres (1883). — Candlesticks and chandeliers of gilded brass by E. Wollenweber.

11 Anteroom

Subdivision of the room by two arches with columns of gray Salzburg marble. Oak panelling and oak furniture.

Decoration: Richly decorated door mountings in all rooms by K. Moradelli. — Cushions and curtains of blue woolen cloth with yellow patterns. — Chandeliers like in all other living quarters of gilded brass by E. Wollenweber, designed by J. Hofmann.

12 Passage

Door to the food-lift from the kitchen.

Fourth Floor

Winding staircase in the Northern Tower compare page 21. The ceiling of the octagonal landing, designed by J. Hofmann in 1881, (Untersberg marble) rising from the center of the stairs seems to grow into the firmament. The banister is formed at the end into a stone dragon, symbolizing the guardian of the tower.

13 Lounge

The lounge of the fourth floor corresponds in form and decoration to the lounge one floor lower. Two marble doors lead to the Singers' Hall; a small door leads to the Southern Tower containing a staircase; to the right is a marble door leading to the gallery of the Throne Hall. On the walls, the Gudrun saga as it is told in the "Edda".

History of construction: Interior designs by J. Hofmann in 1883.

Murals by W. Hauschild in 1884. — *Gudrun saga:* After Sigurd's death, his widow Gudrun, leads a retired life and embroiders tapestry with the great deeds of her ancestors. She is persuaded by her mother of marrying Attila, the King of the Huns. He aspires to gain the Nibelungs' Treasure and invites Gudrun's brothers to his castle. Attila and his Huns attack the Nibelungs, who are all killed. Gudrun takes revenge for her kin: She murders sleeping Attila and throws a torch into the palace where his followers sleep. Gudrun goes into the water to end her life but the waves waft her on to the shores near the castle of King Jonakur. — Western Wall: "After Sigurd's death, Gudrun visits her friend Thora" — "Gudrun and Thora embroidering the heroical deeds of Gudrun's ancestors" — "Attila wooing Gudrun" — "Gudrun's bridal journey with Attila". — Wall with windows: "Attila telling Gudrun his dreams." — Eastern wall: "Attila's messenger at Gunnar's castle" — "Gudrun welcoming her brothers Gunnar and Högni" — "Fight between Nibelungs and Huns" — "Gudrun holding a funeral feast in honour of the dead warriors". — "Gunnar, fettered in the tower" — Entrance side: "Gudrun throwing the torch into the palace" — "Gudrun wafted to distant shores".

Decoration: Benches along the walls with cushions of tooled leather (arms of Bavaria, Wittelsbach, and Schwangau). — Wrought iron chandeliers by K. Moradelli.

14 Singers' Hall

Stimulated by a new production of the Tannhaeuser opera, the King wanted a "Singers' Hall" as part of the future Neuschwanstein castle (compare page 7/8). The final plans combine two predecessors: the Festive Hall (completed in 1867) and the renovated 'historical' Singers' Hall of the Wartburg castle. (Legend tells that a minstrels' competition took place in this Hall at the begin of the 13th century when Hermann ruled as Landgrave of Thuringia). — There is a gallery on the long northern side of the large rectangular hall. Its retaining wall separates a passage from the main room. The passage has a ceiling painted with scrolls bearing the names of minstrels.

In the anteroom, a Good Friday picture. The paintings in the passage itself tell about the adventures of Parzifal's father Gamuret. From the windows, a beautiful view of four lakes, Schwansee, Hopfensee, Forggensee and Bannwaldsee. — In the hall a wood panelled, square ceiling with rich ornamental paintings and the signs of the zodiac. Slanting sides of the ceiling resting on carved wooden supports with symbolic figures; the sorcerer Klingsor appears among others on the alcove. On the small eastern wall, opening to a balcony with view of the courtyard; above, four glass paintings with interlaced ornamentation. In the right corner, a portal that leads to an alcove, which corresponds to a second alcove at the end of the side passage. On the opposite side, stairs lead up to the three arcades of the singers' bower. Stage-like background painting with forest; above, the arcades of a small gallery. The wall of the gallery on the northern side has arcades with marble columns; above, small arcades as gallery sill. Two corbels with figures of Kyot and Flayetanis support the middle balcony. The hall is decorated with scenes of the Parzival saga. — Carved wall benches; coverings interweaved with gold thread. — Chandeliers and candelabra (600 candles altogether) in gilded brass by E. Wollenweber.

History of construction: First sketches done by Chr. Jank in 1868 before the laying of the foundation stone of Neuschwanstein. They were already a copy of the Festive Hall of the Wartburg castle. A later design by the same artist was turned down because the King preferred a set of mural paintings with Parzival motives to a picture series of saints and heroes. First design with Parzival motives by G. Dehn in 1880. Final decoration plans by J. Hofmann in 1882—83.

Mural paintings of the Parzival saga: When Parzival's father Gamuret was killed in a chivalrous adventure, Herzeloide, his widow, educates their son Parzival in isolation. Deeply moved by the sight of a knight, Parzival bids farewell to his mother and heards for King Arthur's court. On the road he meets Sigune, the dead Schianatulander (who was a follower of Gamuret) and the Red Knight, King of Cumberland, whom he kills with his boy's spear. Clad in the Red Knight's armour, Parzival comes to

Gurnemanz who initiates him into knighthood. Later, he frees Queen Kondwiramur from great distress and marries her. Parzival departs to visit his mother again. On his journey, he is received with great honour at Montsalvat, the castle of the Grail, by the ailing King Amfortas. Partaking of a feast, Parzival sees the poisoned bloody spear, the miraculous sword and the Holy Grail, which is carried by the virgin Repane. The knights of the Grail hope that Parzival will release Amfortas from his illness. Their hopes are frustrated since Parzival fails to inquire about the King's ailment. Tortured by nightmares, Parzival is dismissed and scorned the following day. Restlessly, he roams about. On a Good Friday morning, Trevrezent, a hermit, reveals the secret of the Holy Grail to Parzival. He travels on and meets Gawan, the strongest knight of King Arthur's Round Table; Parzival defeats Gawan without recognising him; Parzival volunteers to fight King Gramoflanz. He returns to the Round Table in the company of his half-brother Feirefiz (a son of Gamuret's marriage with Belakane, the Moorish Queen). Kundrie, the Grail's messenger, appears and calls on to him to return to Montsalvat together with his wife Kondwiramur and his son Lohengrin. He saves Amfortas by asking the question. Parzival's youngest son Kardeiz is proclaimed ruler of his hereditary land. Feirefiz and Repane travel to India (their son is later to become the priest King John). Parzival himself becomes the King of the Grail.

Murals in the passage way, anteroom: "Parzival meeting a knight and his family who are on a pilgrimage on Good Friday." In accordance with a romantic wish of the King, this painting had to be finished just on Good Friday, 1884. — On the wall from right to left: "Gamuret in the Moorish town of Patelamunt" — 2) "Gamuret winning Queen Herzeloide and the crown in a tournament" — 3) "Perseverance and Faithfulness" — 4) "Gawan reconciling a couple of lovers, Melianze and Obie" — 5) "Gawan saving a wounded man" — 6) "Moderation". — In the alcove: 7) "Righteousness and Strength". — At the wall with the windows beginning from the right: 8) "Gawan fighting the lion at the enchanted castle of Scorcerer Klingsor" — 9) "Gawan taking a branch from the tree of King Gramoflanz" — 10) "Gawan and Orgeluse's wedding" — 11) Gamuret defeating the enemies of the Moorish Queen Belakane, his first wife" — 12) "Salvation". — The pictures were painted by various artists, A. Spieß (1, 11), J. Munsch (2, 8, 9), F. Piloty (4, 5, 10), W. Kolmsperger (3, 6, maybe 7, 12).

Murals in the Hall by A. Spieß, painted between 1883 and 1884. Southern wall: "Parzival's first encounter with knighthood" — "Parzival bidding farewell to his mother Herzeloide" — "Parzival fighting the Red Knight" — "Parzival marries Kondwiramur" — "Parzival meets Amfortas" — Above the windows of the south side the characters of the Parzival saga on gold background in fields of quatrefoil shape: "Repane and Feirefiz" — "Sigune and Schianatulander" "Ginover and Artus" — "Herzeloide and Gamuret". — In the alcove: "Truth" and "Wisdom" by W. Kolmsperger. — Wall of the balcony: "Parzival at Amfortas' court — Parzival scoffed by the guards", above: "Parzival waited on by women" — "Parzival's dream". — Gallery wall: "Kundrie calls upon Parzival" — "Parzival meet his half-brother Feirefiz" — "Parzival and Trevrezent, the hermit" — "Kundrie's escape". — *Wall of the singer's bower:* above the two doors the Bavarian royal coat of arms with the circumscription "LUDOVICUS II. REX. BAVAR. COM. PALAT." (Ludwig II, King of Bavaria, Count Palatine). — Above the arches of the singers' bower pictures of "Kardeiz" — "Lohengrin" — "Elsa" — "Johannes". — Above in the corners: "Parzival as King of the Grail" — "Lohengrin's departure from the castle of the Grail". Between the ornamental scrolls on the walls of the alcove from top to bottom, left side: "Frau Minne" — "Walther von der Vogelweide" — "Heinrich von Ofterdingen" — "Klingsor" — "Tree of Knowledge". — Right side from top to bottom: "Faith" — "Wolfram von Eschenbach" — "Scriber and Biterolf" — "Reinmar von Zweter" — "Victory of Faith". — Designs of the hall's and passage way's paintings with stylized interlaced ornamentation, flowers and animal symbols by J. Hofmann (co-designer A. Spenger), realised by A. Schultze.

Groundfloor

Kitchen

In the middle of the three-aisled, cross-arched pillar hall, a large hearth and a sideboard; next to it, two meat-chopping blocks. There are two automatically operating spits to roast meat (one small and one large), a built-in oven with space to warm plates, a mortar, and a fish tank. Adjoining, a room for preparing dishes to be served, with built-in cabinet for dishes and a glasspartioned room for the "chef-de-cuisine".

King Ludwig II, 1886.

DATES IN KING LUDWIG II's LIFE

Ludwig II, the last great builder and promoter of the arts from the House of Wittelsbach, was named after his grandfather, King Ludwig I (1825—1848), on whose name-day he was born. Ludwig I was himself a Maecenas who established museums and collections that made Munich a centre of European art. His son, King Maximilian II (1848—1864), married Princess Maria of Prussia in 1842; the two sons of this union were Ludwig II and his brother Otto.

1845, August 25: Ludwig was born at Nymphenburg Palace, Munich.

1861, February 2: Ludwig heard a Wagner opera, "Lohengrin", for the first time.

1864, March 10: Maximilian II died and Ludwig succeeded to the Bavarian throne. — May 4: The King's first meeting with Richard Wagner.

1865, June 10: Première of "Tristan and Isolde" in the Munich Court Theatre. — Dezember 10: Wagner left Munich.

1867, January 22: The King's engagement to Princess Sophie (daughter of Duke Maximilian in Bavaria). — May 31: Visit to the Wartburg. — July 20: Journey to Paris. — October 10: The King's engagement broken off.

1868, June 21: Première of "The Mastersingers of Nuremberg" in the Munich Court Theatre. — First plans for Neuschwanstein.

1869, September 5: Foundation stone of Neuschwanstein Castle laid. — September 22: First performance of "Rhinegold" in the Munich Court Theatre.

1870, June 26: First performance of the "Valkyrie" in the Munich Court Theatre. — September 30: First plan for Linderhof.

1872, May 6: First private performance for the King alone ("Separatvorstellungen"). — May 22: Foundation stone of Festival Theatre in Bayreuth laid.

1873, Purchase of the "Herreninsel" in the Chiemsee.

1874, August 20: Trip to Paris.

1876, February 10: The King present at a court dinner for the last time. — August 6—9, 27—31: The King in Bayreuth ("The Ring of the Nibelung" in the Festival Theatre).

1878, May 21: Foundation stone of Herrenchiemsee Palace laid. — Linderhof completed.

1886, June 8: A gremium of alienists declared Ludwig II to be "mentally deranged" and "incurable" and prevented for life from performing the duties of government.

June 9: Prince Luitpold, son of Ludwig I, became regent for his nephews Ludwig II and Prince Otto, who had been incurably ill since 1871. — Ludwig II ordered the arrest in Neuschwanstein of the Government Commission sent to fetch him.

June 12: A second commission took the King from Neuschwanstein to Berg.

June 13: The King and **Dr**. Gudden found death in lake Starnberg.

June 19: Burial of the King in the Wittelsbach crypt, St. Michaels Church, Munich.

INDEX OF ARTISTS AND CRAFTSMEN

PLATES

13